Blueprints Q&A
STEP 3: PSYCHIATRY

Blueprints Q&A
STEP 3: PSYCHIATRY

SERIES EDITOR:
Michael S. Clement, MD

Fellow, American Academy of Pediatrics
Mountain Park Health Center
Phoenix, Arizona
Clinical Lecturer in Family
 and Community Medicine
University of Arizona College of Medicine
Consultant, Arizona Department
 of Health Services

EDITOR:
James Brian McLoone, MD

Clinical Professor in Psychiatry
University of Arizona
Chairman, Department of Psychiatry
Director, Residency Training and Medical Student
 Clerkship
Good Samaritan Regional Medical Center
Phoenix, Arizona

**Blackwell
Science**

EDITORIAL OFFICES:

Commerce Place, 350 Main Street,
 Malden, Massachusetts 02148, USA

Osney Mead, Oxford OX2 0EL, England

25 John Street, London WC1N 2BS, England

23 Ainslie Place, Edinburgh EH3 6AJ, Scotland

54 University Street, Carlton, Victoria 3053, Australia

OTHER EDITORIAL OFFICES:

Blackwell Wissenschafts-Verlag GmbH,
 Kurfürstendamm 57, 10707 Berlin, Germany

Blackwell Science KK, MG Kodenmacho Building,
 7-10 Kodenmacho Nihombashi, Chuo-ku,
 Tokyo 104, Japan

Iowa State University Press, A Blackwell Science Company,
 2121 S. State Avenue, Ames, Iowa 50014-8300, USA

DISTRIBUTORS:

The Americas
 Blackwell Publishing
 c/o AIDC
 P.O. Box 20
 50 Winter Sport Lane
 Williston, VT 05495-0020
 (Telephone orders: 800-216-2522;
 fax orders: 802-864-7626)

Australia Blackwell Science Pty, Ltd.
 54 University Street
 Carlton, Victoria 3053
 (Telephone orders: 03-9347-0300;
 fax orders: 03-9349-3016)

Outside The Americas and Australia
 Blackwell Science, Ltd.
 c/o Marston Book Services, Ltd., P.O. Box 269
 Abingdon, Oxon OX14 4YN, England
 (Telephone orders: 44-01235-465500;
 fax orders: 44-01235-465555)

Acquisitions: Beverly Copland

Development: Julia Casson

Production: Irene Herlihy

Manufacturing: Lisa Flanagan

Marketing Manager: Toni Fournier

Cover design by Hannus Design

Typeset by Software Services

Printed and bound by Courier-Stoughton

Printed in the United States of America

01 02 03 04 5 4 3 2 1

The Blackwell Science logo is a trade mark of Blackwell Science Ltd., registered at the United Kingdom Trade Marks Registry

Library of Congress Cataloging-in-Publication Data

Blueprints Q & A step 3. Psychiatry / editor,
James McLoone.
   p. ; cm.—(Blueprints Q & A step 3 series)
title: Psychiatry.
   ISBN 0-632-04612-0 (pbk.)
  1. Psychiatry—Examinations, questions, etc.
  2. Physicians—Licenses—United States—Study guides.
   [DNLM: 1. Psychiatry—Examination Questions.
WM 18.2 B6582 2002] I. Title: Psychiatry. II. McLoone,
James Brian. III. Series.
   RC457 .B582 2002
   616.89'0076—dc21   2001004536

Notice: The indications and dosages of all drugs in this book have been recommended in the medical literature and conform to the practices of the general community. The medications described and treatment prescriptions suggested do not necessarily have specific approval by the Food and Drug Administration for use in the diseases and dosages for which they are recommended. The package insert for each drug should be consulted for use and dosage as approved by the FDA. Because standards for usage change, it is advisable to keep abreast of revised recommendations, particularly those concerning new drugs.

CONTRIBUTORS

Lori B. Highberger, MD

Resident in Internal Medicine and Psychiatry

Good Samaritan Regional Medical Center

Phoenix, Arizona

Patricia O. Kirby, MD

Resident in General Psychiatry

Good Samaritan Regional Medical Center

Phoenix, Arizona

James B. McLoone, MD, FAPA

Chairman, Department of Psychiatry

Director, Residence Training and Medical Student Clerkship

Good Samaritan Regional Medical Center

Phoenix, Arizona

Jonathan Zuess, MD

Resident in General Psychiatry

Good Samaritan Regional Medical Center

Phoenix, Arizona

PREFACE

The *Blueprints* Q&A Step 3 series has been developed to complement our core content *Blueprints* books. Each *Blueprints* Q&A Step 3 book (*Medicine, Pediatrics, Surgery, Psychiatry,* and *Obstetrics/ Gynecology*) was written by residents seeking to provide the highest quality of practice review questions simulating the USMLE.

Like the actual USMLE Step 3 exam, this book is divided into different practice settings: community-based health center, office, in-patient facility, and emergency department. Each book covers a single discipline, allowing you to use them during "downtime." Each book contains 100 review cases that cover content typical to the Step 3 USMLE.

Answers are found at the end of each setting, with the correct option highlighted. Accompanying the correct answer is a discussion of why the other options are incorrect. This allows for even the wrong answers to provide you with a valuable learning experience.

Blackwell has been fortunate to work with expert editors and residents—people who have studied for and passed the Boards. They sought to provide you with the very best practice prior to taking the Boards.

We welcome feedback and suggestions you may have about this book or any in the *Blueprints* series. Send to blue@blacksci.com.

All of the authors and staff at Blackwell wish you well on the Boards and in your medical future!

ACKNOWLEDGMENTS

The authors and contributors wish to thank Melissa Hardy for her assistance in typing the manuscript; Dr. Leon Toye for his assistance with the imaging questions; Dr. Andrea Waxman, Dr. Marcelle Leet, and Dr. Christian Cornelius for their reviewing the questions and answers; and the Psychiatry residents and medical students who provided the inspiration for the book.

BLOCK **ONE**

QUESTIONS

Setting 1: Community Health Center

This is a community-based health facility where patients seeking both routine and urgent care are encountered. Many patients are low income; many are ethnic minorities. Several industrial parks and local small businesses send employees there with on-the-job injuries and for employee health screening. There is capability for x-ray films, but CT and MRI must be arranged at other facilities. Laboratory services are available.

QUESTION 1

A 38-year-old Hispanic man was referred by his PCP to the center's psychiatrist for evaluation and treatment of depression. The patient was diagnosed to be HIV positive 3 months ago.

Which one of the following statements about the demographics of HIV/AIDS is correct?

A. 40,000 new infections occur annually in the United States.

B. 25% of new infections among women occur through injection drug use. *heterosexual*

C. More than half of new infections occur among members of minority communities. *Black/Latino*

D. AIDS is the leading cause of death among African-American men between the ages of 25 and 44.

E. All of the above.

QUESTION 2

Upon examination the psychiatrist finds the patient quite distressed about his diagnosis of being HIV positive as well as experiencing ✓ ✓ symptoms of fatigue, anorexia, and insomnia. *SIG E CAPS*

Each of the following statements about the symptoms of depression and HIV infection are true EXCEPT:

A. Vegetative symptoms of depression correlate more closely with the mood disorder than the infection during the early and late phases of HIV.

B. Expected symptoms of distress are typically transient after a patient discovers being HIV positive.

C. Among HIV positive patients, depression is associated with substance abuse, unemployment, and lower education.

D. Specific screening programs increase the likelihood of detecting depression in a primary care setting.

E. The rate of detection of depression in primary care clinics is generally high.

good

QUESTION 3

The psychiatrist decides to treat the patient with an antidepressant medication.

Which of the following statements regarding the selection of an antidepressant medication for an HIV positive patient is INCORRECT?

A. 25–40% of depressed HIV positive patients respond to placebo.

B. 70–80% of depressed HIV positive patients respond to tricyclic antidepressants.

C. 70–80% of depressed HIV positive patients respond to SSRIs.

D. SSRIs are better tolerated.

E. The presence of complex medical comorbidity greatly influences the likelihood of the depression remitting.

QUESTION 4

A 38-year-old unemployed nurse is brought to the center's mental health clinic by her apartment neighbors. They have known her nearly 10 years but since a divorce 3 years ago and living on her own they have noticed a progressive deterioration of her grooming as well as increasing paranoia. One of the neighbors recalls that the patient's father died in a state hospital after a lengthy psychiatric illness and an older brother has been diagnosed with Huntington's disease.

On exam the patient is moderately agitated but oriented to time, person, and place. Her thought process demonstrates loose associations and her insight is impaired. Her physical and neurological examinations are normal.

Each of the following statements about Huntington's disease is true EXCEPT:

A. Most cases present initially with neurologic symptoms.

B. It is transmitted genetically as an autosomal dominant disorder.

C. There is an increased risk of suicide.

D. CNS lesions are found in the caudate nucleus.

E. None of the above.

good

QUESTION 5

A young couple bring their 6-year-old daughter to the center's mental health clinic for treatment of her generalized anxiety. They were referred by their daughter's pediatrician, who could find no physical cause of her symptoms. The parents are adamant that their daughter not be treated with medication.

Which one of the following behavioral treatments has been found helpful for childhood anxiety?

A. Relaxation training

B. Desensitization

C. Modeling

D. Contingency management

E. All of the above

QUESTION 6

A 64-year-old recently widowed janitor has been diagnosed to have terminal pancreatic cancer. In discussing the nature of the illness and his prognosis you should consider which of the following?

A. A fundamental fear of the dying is being abandoned by others.

B. The sequential stages characterizing the response to dying always include denial, anger, bargaining, depression, and acceptance.

C. Cultural and religious background do not influence how individuals respond to dying.

D. All of the above.

E. None of the above.

QUESTION 7

A 38-year-old male parking attendant with schizophrenia is distressed by persistent fears that his job performance is poor, despite multiple commendations and reassurances from his employer and co-workers. He denies hallucinations, ideas of reference, and other psychotic symptoms. For the past few years, he has been prescribed 15 mg of haloperidol daily. Which of the following options for management would NOT be appropriate?

A. Psychodynamic psychotherapy to explore the patient's fears

B. Increasing the dose of haloperidol

C. Checking a blood level of haloperidol

D. Changing to an atypical neuroleptic

E. Cognitive therapy to teach skills to reality test his fears

QUESTION 8

A 38-year-old female with schizoaffective disorder, bipolar type, is currently living in a supervised group home and is followed at the center's mental health clinic. Two months ago she was discharged from a long stay in a state mental hospital and since then has complained of "stress" and difficulty getting to sleep. Today you decide to add carbamazepine to her usual medication regime of olanzapine and thyroid hormone.

One month from now, which of the following adverse effects is the LEAST likely to develop?

A. Breakthrough psychotic symptoms

B. Weight gain

C. Sedation

D. Tardive dyskinesia

E. Nausea

QUESTION 9

A 24-year-old male presents to the center's urgent care area with a 2-year history of increasingly disabling intrusive thoughts about germs. As a result of these thoughts, he says, he spends up to 4 hours a day showering and grooming himself. He recognizes that this is excessive and unreasonable but feels driven to do this to relieve his anxiety. He has never been treated previously for these symptoms. Which of the following would be the most appropriate medication for him?

A. Bupropion

B. Buspirone

C. Olanzapine

D. Clonazepam

E. Sertraline

QUESTION 10

You have been following a young Hispanic man with schizophrenia at the center's mental health clinic over the past 5 years. The patient's mother calls you deeply concerned about her son because he has been talking about harming someone. Which of the following is the single best predictor of violence?

A. A history of violence

B. Paranoid thinking

C. Substance abuse

D. Antisocial personality disorder

E. Head injury

QUESTION 11

A 45-year-old taxi driver is being evaluated by you in the center's urgent care walk-in clinic for insomnia and anxiety. He dates the onset of his symptoms to 1 year ago when he received a concussion in a car accident while working. In spite of a normal MRI scan of his brain taken on the day of the accident he continues to suffer from headaches, dizziness, difficulty concentrating, poor memory, fatigue, insomnia, anxiety, and depressed mood. Once asleep, he is frequently awakened by nightmares about the accident. He feels "jumpy" and is short-tempered with his wife and co-workers. Driving is now an ordeal for him, making him feel tense and irritable. He has missed 6 months of work in the past year because of these symptoms. Which of the following diagnoses would be the LEAST likely?

A. Post-traumatic stress disorder

B. Post-concussional disorder

C. Malingering

D. Acute stress disorder

E. Chronic subdural hematoma

QUESTION 12

As the Medical Director of the center's mental health clinic you are interviewing a psychiatric nurse practitioner who is applying for a position to assist you in the medication clinic. All of the patients assigned to the clinic are receiving psychotropic medications and frequently experience side-effects.

You have composed a quiz to test the applicant's knowledge of medication side-effects. Match the clinical syndrome with the common symptoms.

A. Akathisia

B. Extrapyramidal symptoms

C. Neuroleptic malignant syndrome

D. Tardive dyskinesia

E. Serotonin syndrome

1. Subjective sensation of inner restlessness caused by antipsychotic medications and serotonin reuptake inhibitors.

2. Autonomic instability, dystonia, delirium, fever, and increased creatine kinase.

3. Akinisia, bradykinesia, and masked facies.

4. Tachycardia, hypertension, shivering, and restlessness.

5. Constant, involuntary choreoathetoid movements.

QUESTION 13

A 63-year-old woman with chronic undifferentiated schizophrenia has been successfully maintained on thioridazine. Upon visiting the center's mental health clinic she relates intermittent symptoms over the past several days of palpitations, dizziness, lightheadedness, and syncope.

Thioridazine is associated with prolongation of which specific cardiac conduction interval?

A. QRS interval

B. QT interval

C. T wave interval

D. All of the above

E. None of the above

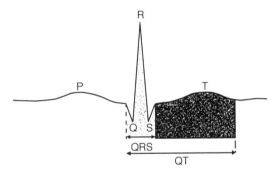

FIGURE 13

QUESTION 14

Prolongation of the QT interval is associated with which arrhythmia?

A. Atrial fibrillation

B. Bradycardia

C. Torsades de pointes

D. All of the above

E. None of the above

QUESTION 15

Each of the following are associated with increased risk of QT interval prolongation EXCEPT:

A. Alcohol abuse

B. Younger age

C. Female gender

D. Electrolyte imbalance

E. None of the above

QUESTION 16

A 39-year-old man with delusional disorder, erotomaniac type admits to you that he is considering doing "something dramatic" that will make the object of his affection, a local celebrity, wish she had paid more attention to him. He refuses to divulge anything further about it.

Which of the following is the most reasonable conclusion to make about this threat and the management of this patient?

A. His threat can be safely dismissed since the patient would not have told the psychiatrist about it if he had really planned to carry it out.

B. The patient appears to be demonstrating thought blocking.

C. Informing patients of the legal limits of confidentiality is foolish since patients are then less likely to tell psychiatrists about their suicidal or homicidal ideation.

D. The psychiatrist may be legally obligated to inform the police.

E. It is a myth that people with mental illness are more dangerous than anyone else.

QUESTION 17

A 44-year-old man refuses to comply with your request to dispose of his firearms. He admits to having thoughts of shooting himself, but states that he wants to keep his guns because he is a gun collector. Important factors in determining the patient's degree of dangerousness to himself would include all of the following EXCEPT:

A. Medical illness

B. Substance abuse

C. Employment history

D. Political party

E. Family history of suicide

QUESTION 18

There is a wide range of racial and ethnic diversity among the patients at the community health center's mental health clinic.

In regards to race and pharmacotherapy each of the following statements is correct EXCEPT:

A. Polymorphisms of aldehyde dehydrogenase and alcohol dehydrogenase are more common in Asians than Caucasians.

B. Asians tend to be more rapid acetylators compared to African-Americans.

C. African-Americans demonstrate a slower metabolism of lithium.

D. All of the above.

E. None of the above.

QUESTION 19

In regards to cultural issues and mental illness each of the following statements is true EXCEPT:

A. The stigma of mental illness is more severe in non-Western societies.

B. Hispanic men tend to equate mental illness with weakness of character.

C. Hispanic women tend to somaticize emotional distress.

D. In the United States race and ethnicity provide for a binding commonality culturally.

E. Asian culture tends to promote a perception of an external locus of control.

QUESTION 20

A 40-year-old male with HIV presents to the center's outpatient clinic with a noticeable elevated mood and increased motor activity. He reports that he has discovered the cure for AIDS and will become famous as a result. He is unable to recite the full date or name of the clinic where he has been coming periodically for treatment over the past 10 years. On physical exam, there are new neurological findings such as slurred speech, coarse tremor in his hands and mouth, hyperactive tendon reflexes, and extensor plantar response. The most likely preliminary diagnosis is

A. Pellagra

B. Neurosyphilis

C. Toxoplasmosis

D. Subacute sclerosis panencephalitis

E. Progressive multifocal encephalopathy

QUESTION 21

A 57-year-old male with schizophrenia, who has been treated with haloperidol decanoate at the center's mental health clinic for the past 20 years, has had a recent onset of frequent lip-pursing, chewing, and grimacing movements. On further evaluation, he is noted to have mild involuntary lateral movements of his jaw, athetoid movement of his hands, and tapping of his feet. Which of the following statements about this condition is TRUE?

A. Patients with mood disorders are at lower risk for it than those with schizophrenia.

B. Lowering the dose of haloperidol may worsen it.

C. Benztropine is an effective treatment for it.

D. Men are at higher risk for it than women.

E. Atypical neuroleptics do not cause it.

BLOCK ONE

ANSWERS

ANSWER 1

E. All of the above.

It is estimated that nearly 900,000 people in the United States are currently infected with HIV. Thirty-three million individuals are infected worldwide.

ANSWER 2

E. The detection of depressive disorders in the HIV infected is complicated and often underdiagnosed. The use of screening methods or on-site psychiatric assessment in HIV clinics can increase early detection of treatable depression.

ANSWER 3

E. With careful assessment and treatment of the depression, patients with complicated HIV infection can achieve substantial improvement in their mood disorders.

ANSWER 4

A. Nearly three-quarters of individuals with Huntington's disease initially present with psychiatric symptoms. Personality changes, mood disorders, anxiety, and finally psychosis are seen in this disease. Transmitted in an autosomal dominant pattern, Huntington's has 100% penetrance. The high association of psychiatric illness and the predictable outcome likely explain the increased suicide risk. The pathophysiology results in decrease in GABA and acetylcholine and a hyperdopaminergic state.

ANSWER 5

E. All of the above.

In general, behavioral methods are helpful in reducing the physiologic sequelae, phobic avoidance, and subjective distress associated with anxiety. Relaxation training can include soothing narrative scripts suitable for this younger patient. Desensitization typically includes graduated exposure to anxiety-provoking stimuli until tolerance develops. Like the exposure techniques, modeling is hierarchical and is often combined with contingency management or operant techniques involving reinforcers.

ANSWER 6

A. Dying alone is a very common fear of the dying. This includes fears that their physician will abandon them.

B. Although the responses to dying often include several if not all the stages listed such is not always the case and there is not necessarily a sequential order to the process.

C. Culture and religion can have a very significant affect as to how people respond to dying, and it is important for the physician to recognize these variables.

ANSWER 7

A. Most clinicians agree that psychodynamic psychotherapy has not been shown to be of significant benefit for patients with schizophrenia. In fact, psychodynamic exploration may destabilize these patients.

B. The patient has a delusion—a fixed false belief—about his work. This symptom may respond, therefore, to an increase in antipsychotic dose.

C. Blood levels of haloperidol can be helpful for assessing compliance.

D. Because of different receptor affinities, atypical neuroleptics can sometimes be effective in patients resistant to typical neuroleptics.

E. Cognitive therapy is being increasingly used for patients with schizophrenia. Cognitive rehabilitation techniques have been shown to improve specific deficits in schizophrenic patients' information processing skills. Cognitive content approaches focus on reality testing of delusional beliefs and masking of auditory hallucinations, and have a role in the care of patients such as this one, who have residual psychotic symptoms while on neuroleptic medication.

ANSWER 8

D. Tardive dyskinesia, though described as occurring with olanzapine, is believed to be much less common than with the typical neuroleptics.

A. Carbamazepine induces hepatic enzymes and can lower levels of other hepatically-metabolized medications, including the antipsychotics. It typically lowers olanzapine levels by 50% or more. Breakthrough psychotic symptoms would therefore be predictable in this case.

B, C, & E. These are all common side effects of both carbamazepine and olanzapine.

ANSWER 9

E. SSRIs like sertraline are considered the first-line medications for OCD.

A. Bupropion has not been studied in OCD. Acting through dopaminergic and noradrenergic mechanisms, it is unlikely to be effective, since the disease appears to be most responsive to serotonergic agents.

B, C, & D. Buspirone, olanzapine, and clonazepam are sometimes used as adjunctive agents in OCD, but they are not first-line treatments

ANSWER 10

A. The single best predictor of future violence is a history of violence.

B, C, D, & E. Each of these choices increases the risk of violence as do specific threats, availability of weapons, and having a motive.

ANSWER 11

D. Acute stress disorder is similar to post-traumatic stress disorder, but by DSM-IV definition, lasts a maximum of 4 weeks.

A & B. With this history, the patient meets criteria for both post-traumatic stress disorder and post-concussional disorder, as proposed by DSM-IV. The latter diagnosis is recognized by most neurologists and is believed to be attributable to diffuse microscopic shearing injuries to axons, which show up better on post-mortem dissection specimens than they do on MRI.

C. Unfortunately, more so than with most injuries, one must consider malingering when assessing work-related injuries.

E. Subdural hematoma may take weeks to accumulate after head injuries and may not show up on brain imaging done at the time of the accident.

ANSWER 12

A. Akathisia

Subjective sensation of inner restlessness caused by antipsychotic medications and serotonin reuptake inhibitors.

C. Neuroleptic malignant syndrome

Autonomic instability, dystonia, delirium, fever, and increased creatine kinase.

B. Extrapyramidal symptoms

Akinesia, bradykinesia, and masked facies.

E. Serotonin syndrome

Tachycardia, hypertension, shivering, and restlessness.

D. Tardive dyskinesia

Constant, involuntary choreoathetoid movements.

ANSWER 13

B. The QT interval is the length of time for the electrical system in the ventricles to depolarize then repolarize. A QT interval in the 350–440 ms range is normal. A QT interval in the 450–500 ms range is of concern and greater than 500 ms has an increased risk of arrhythmia.

ANSWER 14

C. Torsade de pointes is a tachyarrhythmia demonstrating lost cardiac conduction synchrony. It can progress to ventricular fibrillation, which can cause sudden death.

ANSWER 15

B. The elderly are more prone to QT interval prolongation and resultant arrhythmias. Presumably increased risk for coronary disease and the pharmacokinetic differences associated with being elderly are causative factors. Older individuals are also often taking multiple medications, that may themselves potentiate QT prolongation or affect the plasma levels of psychotropics associated with this problem.

ANSWER 16

D. Most states have legislated a duty to warn and to take reasonable precautions to protect identified persons from individuals making threats against them. Such precautions might include voluntary or involuntary hospitalization, notifying the intended victim, notifying the police, adjusting medications, and so on. The origin of this duty to warn and protect derives from the often-mentioned case *Tarasoff v. Regents of the University of California* in the 1970s.

A. Though it seems illogical, patients with homicidal or suicidal ideation often inform others of their intent before committing the act.

B. Thought blocking, a disorder of the thought process, is an abrupt interruption in the train of thought that is beyond conscious control. This patient, on the other hand, appears to be intentionally withholding information.

C. Legal experts recommend informing patients about the legal requirement for health care providers to breach confidentiality when necessary to protect the patient or a third party. Only in rare cases is this likely to reduce patients' willingness to communicate their thoughts about suicide or homicide. Clinical experience has shown that most people have some degree of ambivalence about their suicidal or homicidal thoughts and are likely to be relieved when they inform others of the thoughts and receive help for them.

E. Unfortunately, it is not a myth—people with certain mental illnesses are more likely to commit crimes. Delusional disorders, for example, especially the paranoid, jealous, or erotomaniac types are known to be associated with violent crime.

ANSWER 17

D. Political party is not generally considered to be a risk factor for suicide (at least in democratic countries!).

A, B, C, & E. Presence of physical illness, substance abuse, unemployment, and family history of suicide are all associated with an increased risk for suicide.

ANSWER 18

D. All of the above.

Not surprisingly, recent studies are discovering differences among racial groups in their responses to psychopharmacologic interventions. Dehydrogenase polymorphisms result in a lower tolerance to alcohol in Asians than Caucasians. More rapid or slower metabolism can have an impact on the pharmacokinetics of commonly prescribed medications requiring alterations in dosing practices.

ANSWER 19

D. Actually there is considerable variability within ethnic and racial groups in the United States. A glaring example would include the broad categories of "Black" or "Hispanic" ignoring the various countries and cultures these individuals originate from.

A, B, C, & E. These are considered general tendencies of these multifaceted groupings.

ANSWER 20

B. General paresis, a manifestation of neu-rosyphilis, typically presents as one of three forms: simple dementia, manic type of dementia, or melancholic type dementia. The patient is suffering from manic type and the syndrome is difficult to distinguish from mania seen in bipolar disorder. However, the neurological findings suggest the presence of neurosyphilis.

A. The 3 D's of pellagra, or niacin deficiency, consist of dementia, diarrhea, and dermatitis.

C. Toxoplasmosis, also common in patients with AIDS, presents with signs of delirium, lethargy, fever, and seizures or may present as dementia with focal neurological signs.

D. SSP presents with symptoms of dementia, myoclonus, and ataxia. Hallucinations and mood changes may be present early in illness. Progression of illness is characterized by generalized spastic rigidity, stupor, and eventually coma.

E. Progressive multifocal encephalopathy presents as a progressively worsening dementia associated with hemisensory signs or hemiplegia.

ANSWER 21

B. Reducing the neuroleptic dose may lead to a worsening of tardive dyskinesia. The worsening is usually transient, however.

A. Patients with mood disorders are at higher risk for tardive dyskinesia.

C. Benztropine is effective for neuroleptic-induced acute dystonic symptoms and parkinsonism, but is ineffective for tardive dyskinesia.

D. Women are at higher risk.

E. There are now case reports of tardive dyskinesia and/or tardive dystonia occurring with risperidone, olanzapine, quetiapine, and clozapine. The incidence with these atypical neuroleptics, however, is still believed to be significantly lower than with the typical neuroleptics.

BLOCK TWO

QUESTIONS

Setting 2: Office

Your office is in a primary care generalist group practice located in a physician office suite adjoining a suburban community hospital. Patients are usually seen by appointment. Most of the patients you see are from your own practice and are appearing for regularly scheduled return visits with some new patients. As in most group practices, you will encounter a patient whose primary care is managed by one of your associates; reference may be made to the patient's medical record. You may do some telephone management and you may have to respond to questions about articles in magazines and on TV that will require interpretation. The laboratory and radiology services are complete.

QUESTION 22

A 43-year-old accountant has been in ongoing psychiatric treatment for a recurrent major depressive disorder. The past six weeks her mood disorder has been successfully treated with paroxetine 40 mg daily. At today's return visit she shares with you that she is unable to achieve orgasm. This problem began one week after the paroxetine was increased from 20 mg to 40 mg daily.

The management of antidepressant sexual side effects includes which of the following?

A. Reduce dose of antidepressant.

B. Wait for adaptation.

C. Switch antidepressant.

D. Drug holidays

E. All of the above

QUESTION 23

During the follow-up visit the patient relates she remains unable to experience an orgasm on the higher dose of paroxetine. She prefers to remain on this medication since this is the first time she has not felt depressed in several months.

A pharmacologic antidote for SSRI-related anorgasmia includes which of the following medications?

A. Citalopram

B. Fluoxetine

C. Venlafaxine

D. Bupropion

E. None of the above

QUESTION 24

In considering the use of bupropion as an antidote for SSRI-related sexual side effects, which of the following should be considered?

A. Higher doses of bupropion are associated with seizures.

B. Certain antidepressants co-administered with bupropion may increase its blood level.

C. 15–20% of those prescribed bupropion will stop the medication due to side effects.

D. All of the above.

E. None of the above.

QUESTION 25

A 45-year-old male is referred by his PCP for psychiatric evaluation 1 year after surgical removal of an astrocytoma. His MRI scan is seen below. Based on the location of the lesion, which one of the following symptoms or signs is he most likely to be experiencing?

A. Anhedonia

B. Anosognosia

C. Hallucinations

D. Bulimia

E. Déjà vu

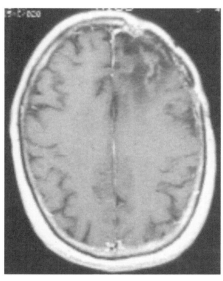

FIGURE 25

QUESTION 26

An 8-year-old girl is referred with her mother to you as the group's consulting child psychiatrist specializing in pain management. The girl is about to undergo a series of surgical procedures to correct a congenital back deformity.

Which of the following is true regarding hypnosis and pain management?

A. Hypnosis is effective in controlling even severe surgical pain.

B. Hypnosis works through muscle relaxation and perceptual alteration.

C. Hypnosis is especially effective in comforting children who are in pain.

D. All of the above.

E. None of the above.

QUESTION 27

A 16-year-old female previously diagnosed with bulimia claims that she no longer binges or vomits. Her parents, however, do not believe her and ask her PCP to assess the situation.

Which of the following tests would be useful for this purpose?

A. Stool bicarbonate level

B. Serum albumin level

C. Plasma prolactin level

D. Serum gastrin level

E. Serum amylase level

QUESTION 28

A 63-year-old retired nurse has been followed by you as the group's psychiatrist for a recurrent major depressive disorder. This past decade she has responded to a variety of selective serotonin reuptake inhibitors. Her physical health has started to decline and she is now also taking medications for hypertension, hyperlipidemia, and gout. Both you and her internist are concerned with drug–drug interactions.

Referring to the following table, match the lettered antidepressants with the numbered rows best reflecting the relative inhibitory effects for the cytochrome P450 isoenzymes of each medication.

+ = mild   ++ = moderate   +++ = strong

  − = no significant inhibitory effect.

A. Citalopram

B. Nefazodone

C. Fluoxetine

D. All of the above

E. None of the above

	3A4	2D6	1A2	2C9
1	−	+	+	−
2	+++	+	−	−
3	+	+++	+	++

QUESTION 29

A 75-year-old man has been seen in your office for the past 2 years. He has just lost his wife of 40 years to breast cancer and reports being very depressed most days for the past month. Which of the following symptoms would suggest the greatest risk of suicide danger in this type of patient?

A. Decreased sleep

B. Poor appetite

C. Hopelessness

D. Command hallucinations

E. Physical illness

QUESTION 30

A 54-year-old man is followed in the group practice by an internist for diabetes and by you for psychotherapy. During a psychotherapy session with you the patient scowls and complains that he has been taken advantage of by every person to whom he has ever been emotionally close. When you comment that many people who have been taken advantage of by others might feel angry, the patient denies ever having felt angry. He then says, "You're just like everybody else—trying to dismiss me because you're sick and tired of me."

Which of the following defense mechanisms is the patient displaying?

A. Suppression

B. Displacement

C. Reaction formation

D. Projection

E. Identification

QUESTION 31

A 78-year-old widow with long-standing diabetes and hypertension is referred by her internist to you for evaluation and treatment of depression. She had a TIA 4 years ago. A brain MRI demonstrated lesions typical of microvascular disease.

Each of the following are common findings in vascular depression EXCEPT:

A. Frontal lobe syndrome

B. Focal neurologic signs

C. Abnormal MRI

D. Incontinence

E. None of the above

QUESTION 32

Which of the following treatment approaches for vascular depression is NOT indicated?

A. Antidepressant pharmacotherapy

B. Vascular prophylaxis

C. Management of neurologic symptoms

D. Personal care assistance

E. Psychodynamic psychotherapy

QUESTION 33

A 10-year-old mentally retarded boy is referred by you to the group's pediatrician for a general medical examination. Which of the following statements are true regarding the psychosocial consequences of mental retardation?

A. The prevalence of associated mental disorders is greater in the mentally retarded than the general population.

B. The mentally retarded are at greater risk for sexual abuse.

C. Social stressors are particularly problematic in this population.

D. All of the above.

E. None of the above.

QUESTION 34

A recently divorced psychiatrist doing locum tenens work in your group practice has been seeing a younger patient for psychotherapy the past 3 months. Over the course of several sessions they share a mutual physical attraction to each other and decide to meet socially outside the office. They eventually become sexually intimate at her apartment.

Each of the following statements regarding this situation is true EXCEPT:

A. Malpractice claims based on sexual misconduct are relatively common.

B. Sexual activity with a patient demonstrates mismanagement of the transference and countertransference.

C. Sexual activity with a patient is always considered a dereliction of duty.

D. All of the above.

E. None of the above.

QUESTION 35

A 14-year-old boy is accompanied by his father for a psychiatric consultation. Over the past 6 months the boy has been washing his hands excessively and preoccupied with concerns that something bad will happen to his father even though he is in good health.

The differential diagnosis of obsessive–compulsive disorder (OCD) includes which of the following?

A. Developmental rituals of childhood

B. Stereotypies in mentally retarded persons

C. Major depression

D. All of the above

E. None of the above

QUESTION 36

Each of the following statements regarding the treatment of OCD is true EXCEPT:

A. Exposure with response prevention is the behavioral treatment of choice for adults with OCD.

B. Prolonged exposure in children may reinforce the anxiety.

C. Family therapy is worthwhile.

D. Serotonin reuptake inhibitors are effective in the treatment of OCD.

E. Long-term maintenance treatment is typically not required.

QUESTION 37

Over the course of several months you have successfully assisted a 33-year-old patient in adjusting to the death of her mother. During the course of psychotherapy the patient reveals that she is prone to extreme fatigue, crying spells, angry outbursts, and insomnia several days before the onset of her menstrual period. She has experienced these symptoms for several years.

Which of the following medications would be the best intervention for this patient?

A. Nortriptyline

B. Amitriptyline

C. Fluoxetine

D. All of the above

E. None of the above

QUESTION 38

An 18-year-old woman is accompanied to a primary care physician in your group by her mother, who is concerned that the patient is avoiding social contacts away from the immediate family. The patient lives with her parents and has worked only intermittently since graduating from high school. Further questioning of the patient reveals no typical symptoms of a clinical depression. In fact, the patient seems to enjoy her day-to-day activities at home.

Which of the following characteristics of this particular patient are typical of someone with a social anxiety disorder?

A. Her age

B. Being female

C. Living with parents

D. All of the above

E. None of the above

QUESTION 39

Which one of the following conditions has an increased comorbidity with social anxiety disorder?

A. Substance abuse

B. Depression

C. Anxiety disorders

D. Chronic medical illness

E. All of the above

QUESTION 40

Which one of the following is indicated in the treatment of social anxiety disorder?

A. Phenelzine

B. Paroxetine

C. Cognitive-behavioral therapy

D. All of the above

E. None of the above

QUESTION 41

A 37-year-old female with a treatment-refractory mood disorder is referred for psychiatric consultation. She draws a graph for you depicting the course of her mood since the onset of her illness 3 years ago. Based on this graph, which of the following diagnoses is the most likely?

A. Cyclothymic disorder

B. Bipolar I disorder, with seasonal pattern

C. Bipolar II disorder, with seasonal pattern

D. Bipolar I disorder, with rapid cycling

E. Bipolar II disorder, with rapid cycling

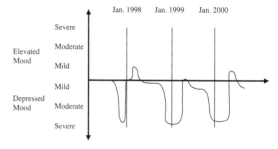

FIGURE 41

QUESTION 42

A single parent of a 16-year-old girl accompanies her daughter to your group's family practice physician. The daughter is mentally retarded with an IQ in the 60–65 range and recently has been showing an interest in boys.

Each of the following is a true statement about sexuality and mental retardation EXCEPT:

A. Some states in the United States maintain legislation for sterilization of the mentally retarded.

B. The most profoundly retarded tend to show little interest in sexual activity with others.

C. Sexual behavior may be used in an attempt to gain acceptance in a peer group.

D. Indiscriminate sexual behavior is a characteristic of mentally retarded persons.

E. Mild and moderately retarded adolescents are at risk for sexual exploitation.

QUESTION 43

Which of the following statements would be the best advice from the family practitioner to the parents of this mentally retarded adolescent girl regarding her sexuality?

A. Encouragement of relationships with others to teach social skills.

B. Provide specific instruction about sexual activity.

C. Consider the pros and cons of contraception.

D. All of the above.

E. None of the above.

QUESTION 44

A 19-year-old college student revealed to her family practice physician in your group practice a history of sexual abuse by her father at age 6. Her father has since died but she remains conflicted by what happened.

The repercussions of childhood sexual abuse in women include each of the following EXCEPT:

A. Increased likelihood of victimization as an adult

B. Residual sense of helplessness

C. Sense of guilt in other areas of life

D. Identification with the aggressor

E. None of the above

QUESTION 45

Which one of the following statements about the gender of the therapist for a sexual abuse patient is TRUE?

A. Males are more likely to be referred to a male therapist.

B. Female patients show greater responsiveness to therapy.

C. More experienced therapists have better therapeutic results.

D. There is little outcome difference by gender of therapist for short-term psychotherapy.

E. All of the above.

QUESTION 46

Which one of the following psychiatric disorders is frequently associated with a history of sexual abuse?

A. Borderline personality disorder

B. Bulimia nervosa

C. Conversion disorder

D. Factitious disorder

E. All of the above

QUESTION 47

The parents and 18-month-old sister of a 15-year-old girl recently diagnosed with schizophrenia attend a psychiatric appointment along with her. The parents ask about the cause of the illness, its prognosis, and the risk that the patient's younger sister will develop it. Correct statements regarding these issues would include all of the following EXCEPT:

A. Studies suggest that genetic influences outweigh environmental influences in the causation of schizophrenia.

B. No well-controlled study indicates that family rearing patterns have any influence on whether the offspring will develop schizophrenia.

C. The risk that the patient's baby sister will develop schizophrenia is approximately 50%.

D. Patients with a sudden onset of symptoms have a better prognosis.

E. Family therapy has been shown to be effective in preventing relapse.

QUESTION 48

A young couple has been concerned about the delayed development of their 30-month-old son and ask their pediatrician for a referral to a child psychiatrist. After a thorough psychiatric examination, you inform them that their son may either have Asperger's syndrome or autism.

Each of the following characteristics differentiates Asperger's syndrome from autistic disorder EXCEPT:

A. Both have impairment in social interaction.

B. Both have repetitive behavior patterns.

C. Both have delays in speech development.

D. Both have genetic influences.

E. Both are more common in boys.

QUESTION 49

A 73-year-old man is accompanied by his spouse to his primary care physician in your group for evaluation of personality changes, trouble finding words and recognizing other relatives, and declining recent memory over the past 6 months. Although the patient volunteers little information, he is alert throughout the examination.

These symptoms are most typical of which one of the following clinical syndromes:

A. Delirium

B. Dementia

C. Depression

D. Schizophrenia

E. None of the above

QUESTION 50

Physical examination, electrocardiography, and routine laboratory studies including thyroid function testing are unremarkable.

Each of the following is likely to be found in the older patient with early to mid-dementia EXCEPT:

A. A Mini-Mental State Examination score of 16

B. Mild atrophy of CT of the head

C. Marked slowing of EEG

D. Concrete thinking

E. None of the above

QUESTION 51

A 39-year-old female is referred by her gynecologist with complaints of anxiety. She worries that she may lose her job because her co-workers are talking about her and laughing behind her back. She admits she has very few friends or confidants because she believes "people cannot be trusted." She refuses to give any further history because she worries the information will be used "against her." When the receptionist tried to compliment her appearance, she became angry and felt insulted. The most likely diagnosis is:

A. Borderline personality disorder

B. Schizotypal personality disorder

C. Narcissistic personality disorder

D. Paranoid personality disorder

E. None of the above

QUESTION 52

A 50-year-old female who has been seen in your office for the past 5 years has an abrupt personality change in the past week. She is on warfarin for atrial fibrillation, but is otherwise physically healthy. On exam she has bruising along her right temple. You choose to order an emergent computed tomography (CT) of the brain over magnetic resonance imaging (MRI) of the brain for which of the following reasons?

A. MRI exposes the patient to more radiation than CT.

B. CT can obtain thinner slices than MRI.

C. MRI requires iodinated contrast be given, which can cause renal failure.

D. CT obtains better images of the posterior fossa.

E. None of the above.

QUESTION 53

A 78-year-old widowed steelworker is accompanied to your office by his daughter. They were referred by her father's internist, who recently discovered a coin lesion on x-ray of the patient's chest. The patient is refusing further evaluation and his internist is requesting psychiatric consultation regarding the patient's decision-making capacity.

In regard to the psychiatric evaluation, which one of the following is the best approach?

A. Obtain a comprehensive history from the daughter while the patient waits in the lobby.

B. Start the assessment with direct questioning to the patient regarding his cognitive functioning.

C. Attempt to engage the patient to express his feelings concerning the situation.

D. All of the above.

E. None of the above.

QUESTION 54

As the evaluation of the patient's decision-making capacity progresses, you perform a Mini-Mental State Examination.

The use of this diagram includes which of the following?

A. Assessment of the patient's construction capabilities

B. A score of 1 if *all* 10 angles are present and 2 angles intersect

C. Ignoring tremor and rotation

D. All of the above

E. None of the above

QUESTION 55

A mother brings her 9-year-old son into your outpatient office concerned that he has been behind in his reading, writing, and arithmetic classes. Her son requires constant supervision when performing simple tasks such as getting ready for bed or eating meals. Based on IQ testing he has moderate mental retardation. On physical exam, you note that he has a high, broad forehead and a long thin face. Prior chromosomal testing for Down syndrome was negative. Which of the following chromosomal abnormalities would be the most likely cause of his mental retardation?

A. One or more extra X chromosomes

B. Expanded trinucleotide repeats on the X chromosome

C. Deletion of chromosome 15

D. X-linked deficiency of hypoxanthine-guanine phosphoribosyltransferase

E. None of the above

QUESTION 56

A 10-year-old boy already diagnosed with attention-deficit hyperactivity disorder is being evaluated for behavioral problems. These have consisted of rude behavior in class, church, and at home and have been increasing in severity for the last 2 years despite treatment with methylphenidate. He makes faces at others and talks out of turn, saying nonsense phrases, such as, "Hey, hey, hey, la, la, la!" On questioning, he blushes, squirms uncomfortably in his seat, and says he doesn't mean to do these things. He blinks and licks his lips repeatedly, clenches and unclenches his fists, sticks out his tongue, and clears his throat every few minutes. In educating the parents and their child about this condition, which of the following statements would be INCORRECT?

A. Decreasing the dose of methylphenidate may be helpful.

B. It is strongly associated with both ADHD and OCD.

C. Psychotherapy is generally ineffective for it.

D. Clonidine is used to treat it.

E. It may be exacerbated by treatment with dopamine antagonists like haloperidol.

QUESTION 57

A single 40-year-old male mechanic presents to your outpatient office with complaints of depression. He states that he has few friends or confidants as supports. He prefers to spend time alone and avoids developing any close relationships. He has no particular hobbies nor does he engage in any pleasurable activities outside of his work. He has often been criticized by co-workers for not being more interactive with others. On evaluation, he appears cold, detached, and shows little emotional reaction. What is the most likely diagnosis?

A. Schizotypal personality disorder

B. Schizoid personality disorder

C. Avoidant personality disorder

D. Obsessive–compulsive personality disorder

E. None of the above

QUESTION 58

A 19-year-old woman with a history of panic disorder and agoraphobia is referred to you for treatment. She states she has previously had trials of several SSRIs but was unable to tolerate their side effects. She has also had a full course of cognitive-behavioral therapy with little effect. The only treatment that has been helpful, she says, is alprazolam 2 mg tid. She has been on this for 6 months and ran out 2 weeks ago. She has been extremely anxious since then. She is on vacation from another state and because of this she has been unable to see her regular doctor for a refill. She denies any history of substance abuse. Which of the following would NOT be an appropriate part of management at this time?

A. Trial of an SSRI, starting with an extremely low dose.

B. Asking her to wait in the waiting room, and without her knowledge, calling her previous psychiatrist to verify her history.

C. Prescribing alprazolam 2 mg tid.

D. Prescribing alprazolam 0.5 mg qid.

E. Prescribing clonazepam in an equivalent dose.

QUESTION 59

A 41-year-old male is referred for psychiatric consultation in your outpatient office. He draws a graph depicting the course of his mood since the onset of his illness 5 years ago as depicted below. Which one of the following statements about his condition is TRUE?

A. Double depression is rare, occurring in less than 1% of all depressed patients.

B. The risk of suicide is generally lower in double depression than in episodic major depressive disorder, since patients with double depression tend to become accustomed to feeling depressed.

C. Double depression responds just as well to standard antidepressant treatments as does major depressive disorder.

D. The term "double depression" refers to the combination of major depressive disorder and a depressive disorder due to substance abuse.

E. Risk of a bipolar outcome is higher in double depression than in episodic major depressive disorder.

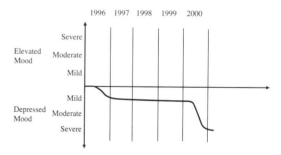

FIGURE 59

QUESTION 60

A 69-year-old female is brought to your outpatient office for a consultation by her husband. He has noticed problems with her memory of recent events. Her mood has been good and she has no other symptoms of depression. In evaluating this patient which of the following are likely present if Alzheimer's dementia is the correct diagnosis?

A. Changes in personality

B. Decline in performance of complex tasks

C. Difficulty or inability to make decisions when given many options

D. All of the above

E. None of the above

QUESTION 61

A 72-year-old man whom you have diagnosed with Alzheimer's dementia would like to pursue treatment to prevent further decline in his cognitive functions. In discussing the options that are available to him, the one that is least likely to be beneficial based on current studies is?

A. Reality orientation

B. Gingko biloba

C. Donepezil

D. Reminiscence therapy

E. Selegiline

QUESTION 62

A family practice colleague in your group recently saw an effeminate 8-year-old boy in his office and asks you to explain the concepts of gender identity and gender role.

Each of the following statements regarding gender identity is correct EXCEPT:

A. It is the internalized sense of maleness or femaleness.

B. Begins to evolve in early childhood.

C. Is influenced by parental attitudes, expectations, and behaviors.

D. Tends to be firmly established after adolescence.

E. Is influenced by cultural factors.

QUESTION 63

A 33-year-old woman was referred by her PCP to you for grief counseling. Three weeks earlier her husband died tragically in an automobile accident.

The initial psychological symptoms associated with grief include each of the following EXCEPT:

A. Despair

B. Protest

C. Increased socialization

D. Disbelief

E. Preoccupation with the deceased

QUESTION 64

As the group's consulting psychiatrist you are providing an inservice to your PCP colleagues on sexual dysfunctions. You show them the enumerated sexual response phases depicted on the graph below and ask them to select the associated sexual disorders in men.

A. Sexual aversion

B. Premature ejaculation

C. Retrograde ejaculation

D. Erectile dysfunction

E. Priapism

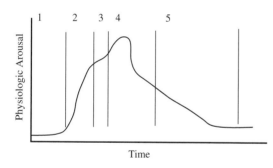

FIGURE 64

QUESTION 65

A 26-year-old single woman is referred to you for psychiatric consultation by her gynecologist for evaluation and treatment of symptoms of anger outbursts, impulsivity, and cutting upon herself to relieve tension.

Regarding the pharmacologic treatment of personality disorders each of the following is true EXCEPT:

A. Selective serotonin reuptake inhibitors have helped mediate impulsivity.

B. Phenelzine has demonstrated efficacy against anger and hostility.

C. Behavioral dyscontrol may respond to carbamazepine.

D. All of the above.

E. None of the above.

BLOCK TWO

ANSWERS

ANSWER 22

E. All of the above.

Antidepressant sexual side effects appear to be dose related. Adaptation to the sexual side effects occurs when the complaints are mild and more often to delayed orgasm than arousal or libido complaints. One- or two-day "drug holidays" can be an effective strategy with antidepressants that have a shorter half-life such as paroxetine or sertraline. Switching antidepressants may eliminate or reduce the side effects but may also cause a recurrence of the mood disorder.

ANSWER 23

D. Bupropion is an antidepressant devoid of serotonergic activity. Its increase of both norepinephrine and dopamine probably improves the SSRI-related side effects.

A, B, & C. Citalopram, fluoxetine, and venlafaxine each have SSRI properties.

ANSWER 24

D. All of the above.

Studies have shown that doses up to 225 mg/day of bupropion improve a variety of SSRI-related side effects. Doses above 450 mg/day are associated with a higher incidence of seizures. Both fluoxetine and paroxetine may inhibit cytochrome P450 3A4 and 2D6 hepatic isoenzymes, which could increase the blood level of bupropion. Bupropion itself can cause a variety of undesirable side effects, causing the patient to stop the medication.

ANSWER 25

A. Anhedonia or the inability to experience pleasure typical of a clinical depression may be seen with a lesion in virtually any location in the brain, but it is especially common with left frontal lobe disease.

B. Anosognosia, or ignorance of illness, is usually associated with nondominant parietal lobe disease.

C. Hallucinations are more often associated with temporal or occipital lobe lesions than with frontal ones.

D. Eating disorders are sometimes associated with ventromedial hypothalamic lesions or with bilateral temporal lesions (as part of the Klüver–Bucy syndrome).

E. Déjà vu is sometimes associated with temporal lobe lesions.

ANSWER 26

D. All of the above.

The two primary mechanisms found useful with hypnosis and related techniques include muscle relaxation and a combination of perceptual alterations and cognitive distraction. As a group, children are more hypnotizable than adults, and because their imaginations are so strong, separate relaxation strategies are often not necessary.

ANSWER 27

E. Serum amylase levels are commonly elevated in patients who binge and vomit, reflecting parotid gland hypertrophy. Amylase levels decline in recovering bulimics as they refrain from vomiting. They are thus used to verify reduction in vomiting in patients who deny purging.

A. Stool bicarbonate level is a rarely ordered test used in the differential diagnosis of diarrhea.

B. Serum albumin level does not correlate with vomiting in bulimia.

C. Plasma prolactin levels are sometimes ordered by psychiatrists to assess amenorrhea and galactorrhea in patients on dopamine blocking medications. A variety of other medications and medical conditions also cause hyperprolactinemia.

D. Serum gastrin levels are used to diagnose gastrinoma in cases of severe peptic ulceration (Zollinger–Ellison syndrome).

ANSWER 28

A. Citalopram: Row 1. *In vitro* studies indicate this SSRI has the least inhibitory effect on these cytochrome P450 isoenzymes.

B. Nefazodone: Row 2.

C. Fluoxetine: Row 3. Fluoxetine's metabolite has moderate to strong inhibitory effects on 3A4, 2D6, and 2C9 isoenzymes as well.

ANSWER 29

D. Command hallucinations suggest a severe risk of suicide since the hallucination may instruct the patient to harm himself.

A, B, & E. These answers may indicate the severity of the depression but not the severity of suicidal risk.

C. Hopelessness may indicate a passive suicidal ideation but command hallucinations are the most worrisome symptoms in this list.

ANSWER 30

D. In projection, unacceptable inner impulses, thoughts, or affects are attributed to entities outside the self. This patient appears to be attributing to the psychiatrist the feeling of anger, which he denies in himself.

A. Suppression is the conscious decision to withhold attention from a conflict for the time being, until a more suitable time arrives to deal with it. The patient's denial of anger and his lifelong pattern of unresolved conflicts suggests that he is not using a conscious defense mechanism such as suppression, but rather, an unconscious one.

B. Displacement is the shifting of feelings related to one concept or object to another one which is similar to it in some way. This process distances the feeling from its source and reduces one's anxiety in dealing with it.

C. Reaction formation is the transformation of an unacceptable impulse into its opposite. For example, a person who hates another person might act excessively loving toward them.

E. In identification, the person sees qualities of others within themselves.

ANSWER 31

E. Late life depression associated with vascular disease typically occurs concurrently with focal or diffuse neurologic signs, which would be expectedly highlighted on brain imaging. Lesions in the basal ganglia and prefrontal areas are common.

ANSWER 32

E. Goal-oriented psychotherapy is indicated in this patient group rather than psychodynamic psychotherapy. Patients with impairment in executive functions may benefit from counseling to assist in organizing their activities.

ANSWER 33

D. All of the above.

Associated mental disorders are 3–4 times greater in mentally retarded persons and the full range of disorders may be diagnosed. They are also at greater risk for exploitation and sexual and physical abuse. By definition, adaptive behavior is impaired in mental retardation, and these individuals are especially prone to difficulty coping with stress.

ANSWER 34

A. Sexual activity between a psychiatrist and his or her patient is grounds for malpractice and is contrary to the ethics of the specialty. Nonetheless malpractice claims based on sexual misconduct are relatively uncommon. In some jurisdictions sexual activity between a mental health professional and his or her patient is a criminal offense.

ANSWER 35

D. All of the above.

The rituals associated with OCD are usually more severe and persistent and have a later age of onset than normal developmental rituals. Mentally retarded, autistic, and developmentally delayed children may demonstrate stereotypies resembling OCD rituals. The morbid ruminations of major depression are typically accompanied by other depressive symptoms.

ANSWER 36

E. Long-term therapy is typically required for OCD. This ideally would include pharmacotherapy with a serotonergic agent and combined behavioral and cognitive psychotherapies. The younger patient may benefit from family therapy to educate parents and siblings about the illness and to help develop a balance of empathy without over-involvement in the child's rituals.

ANSWER 37

C. Fluoxetine.

Approximately 5% of women suffer from premenstrual syndrome (PMS) or premenstrual dysphoric disorder (PMDD). The selective reuptake inhibitors (SSRIs) have proven to be the best psychotropic intervention. Tricyclic agents such as answers A and B are not nearly as effective. Some studies have shown that SSRIs are 7 times more effective than placebo. The response is often much quicker than seen in treating depression and may only require taking the medication a few days before the onset of symptoms with discontinuation when menses begin.

ANSWER 38

D. All of the above.

Social anxiety disorder or social phobia typically has its onset in adolescence. Most studies have found a slightly higher rate of this condition in females. Quality of life for people with social anxiety disorder is lowest in social, occupational, and financial dependency.

ANSWER 39

E. All of the above.

Comorbidity is the rule rather than the exception and social anxiety disorder usually precedes the comorbid condition.

ANSWER 40

D. All of the above.

The monamine oxidase inhibitor phenelzine and the selective serotonin reuptake inhibitors such as paroxetine are efficacious in the treatment of social anxiety disorder. Due to safety considerations the SSRIs have replaced the MAOIs as a first-line pharmacologic intervention. Several cognitive-behavioral psychotherapy strategies including exposure, cognitive restructuring, relaxation, and social skills training have proven helpful for social anxiety disorder patients as well.

ANSWER 41

C. The patient has recurrent major depressive episodes and hypomanic episodes, thus meeting the definition of bipolar II disorder. There is also a regular temporal relationship between the onset of major depressive episodes and a particular time of year. Full remissions, or a change from depression to mania, also occur regularly at a particular time of year, in her case in the spring. Her mood disorder thus also demonstrates a seasonal pattern.

A. In cyclothymic disorder, numerous episodes of depressive symptoms that do not meet full criteria for major depressive disorder, and numerous episodes of hypomania are present over a period of at least 2 years. No major depressive episode may occur in the first 2 years of the illness—if it does, the diagnosis is bipolar II disorder, as in this case.

B & D. To make the diagnosis of bipolar I disorder, a full manic episode must occur at some point in the illness.

D & E. Rapid cycling is defined as four or more mood episodes in a year.

ANSWER 42

D. Uninhibited or indiscriminate sexual behavior, sexual immaturity, and lacking sexual interests altogether are stereotypes associated with mental retardation. This patient's IQ classifies her as mildly mentally retarded. This group and many moderately retarded persons may have normal pubertal development, sexual interests, and sexual identities. Similar to other adolescents, sexual behavior may serve as a means to demonstrate self-importance or gain acceptance from peers.

ANSWER 43

D. All of the above.

Socialization skills are a prerequisite to facilitate the development of normal sexual identification. The usual sources of sex education in schools, peer discussions, and reading material are often not available to mentally retarded persons and should be provided by trusted others.

ANSWER 44

D. Women survivors of childhood sexual abuse are more likely to establish relationships with abusive men while male survivors of abuse tend to identify with the aggressor and repeat the behavior.

ANSWER 45

E. Studies of this complex topic suggest each of the statements is true.

ANSWER 46

E. Certainly each of these disorders can occur independent of a past history of sexual abuse. Nonetheless, there is an increased association with these conditions as well as sexual disorders and dissociative states with a history of childhood sexual abuse.

ANSWER 47

C. The risk that a non-twin sibling of a patient with schizophrenia will also develop the illness is only about 10%. The risk to a *monozygotic twin* of the patient, however, is about 50%.

A. Studies show that the members of monozygotic twin pairs, who are adopted and raised by nonbiological parents, have the same incidence of schizophrenia as their twins who were not adopted out, but who were instead kept and raised by their biological parents. These studies suggest that the environmental influence is less significant than the genetic one.

B. This is also true.

D. Features associated with a good prognosis in schizophrenia include good premorbid functioning, obvious precipitating factors, sudden onset of symptoms, and delirium-like confusion or perplexity at the height of the episode. Poor outcome, by contrast, is predicted by poor premorbid functioning, no precipitant, insidious onset, negative symptoms, and an early age of onset.

E. Family therapy reduces the relapse rate in the first year by about 40%.

ANSWER 48

C. Significant abnormalities in speech development are not typical of children with Asperger's syndrome. There are abnormalities to their eventual communication patterns. These include constricted intonation and verbosity. Asperger's syndrome (AS) is one of several pervasive developmental disorders. Its etiology is unknown but brain structure and genetic abnormalities are thought to play a role. Present in both autism and AS, the genetic component is seemingly stronger in AS. Both conditions require multidisciplinary interventions including highly structured educational programs and extensive parental involvement.

ANSWER 49

B. Dementia is always accompanied by some memory impairment with one or more cognitive deficits such as aphasia, aproxia, or agnosia.

A. Although delirium also involves memory impairment, this occurs in a state of clouded consciousness.

C. The pseudodementia of depression is typically accompanied with pervasive affective changes and the patient is typically quite concerned with the cognitive loss.

D. The onset of schizophrenia is typically much earlier in life and marked by psychotic symptoms such as delusions and hallucinations.

ANSWER 50

C. An EEG obtained early in the course of dementia is typically unremarkable.

A. The Folstein Mini-Mental State Exam assesses orientation, registration, attention, calculation, recall, language, and construction skills. The maximum score is 30, so a score of 16 strongly suggests significant cognitive and memory impairment typical of dementia.

B. Mild atrophy of the brain is consistent with normal aging and patients with dementia are often unable to abstract.

D. Concrete thinking is typical.

ANSWER 51

D. Paranoid personality disorder is character-ized by a persistent pattern of distrust and suspiciousness of others. These individuals suspect, without basis, that others are exploit-ing, harming, or deceiving them. There is a persistent fear that personal information will be used against them. These individuals may display anger at others they perceive as insulting or hostile toward them.

A. Borderline personality disorder is character-ized by a pattern of instability of interper-sonal relationships, self-image, and affects. These individuals may react to minor stim-uli with anger, but anger is not typically associated with pervasive suspiciousness.

B. Schizotypal personality disorder is charac-terized by a persistent pattern of social and interpersonal deficits. Although paranoid ideation and suspiciousness may be pres-ent, there are typically symptoms of magical thinking, unusual perceptual experiences, and odd thinking and speech.

C. Narcissistic personality disorder is character-ized by a persistent pattern of grandiosity, need for admiration, and lack of empathy. Suspicious feelings or expressions of anger stems from a fear of having imperfections or flaws revealed.

ANSWER 52

E. The emergent diagnosis that needs to be evaluated in this patient is traumatic intracra-nial bleeding. CT is preferred to detect bony fractures and acute bleeds, it does not require contrast for these purposes, and can be obtained faster than MRI in most facilities.

A. MRI uses magnetic fields, not radiation (x-rays).

B. MRI can obtain thinner slices and is able to distinguish white and gray matter.

C. MRI uses gadolinium, not iodinated con-trast. Gadolinium can cause anaphylaxis in some patients, but is not associated with contrast induced renal failure.

D. Due to the predominance of bone in the posterior fossa the CT scan has interference in its images of soft tissue, which is why MRI is preferred for evaluating lesions in this area.

ANSWER 53

C. A conversational approach allows the patient to see the psychiatrist as an ally. Considerable valuable information about the patient's cognitive and reasoning ability can be obtained in the early stages of the interview by the less threatening approach of indirect questioning. Favoring the daughter's input, especially if done away from the patient, may foster paranoia and distrust in the patient.

ANSWER 54

D. All of the above.

The Folstein Mini-Mental State Exam is a convenient easy to score cognitive functioning screening tool. Specific areas assessed include orientation, registration, attention and calculation, recall, language, and construction by copying the diagram correctly. The maximum score for the complete exam is 30.

ANSWER 55

B. Fragile X syndrome is the second most common cause of mental retardation after Down syndrome. It is caused by a fragile site on the X chromosome consisting of expanded repeats of the CGG triplet. Only female carriers can transmit the disease. Affected individuals are characterized by dysmorphic facial features and anorchidism.

A. 47XXY is the classic karyotype of Klinefelter's syndrome, secondary to nondisjunction during meiosis in either parent. Classic presentation is a tall male with disproportionately long legs and underdeveloped gonads. Mental retardation is possible; however, most affected individuals have normal IQ.

C. Prader–Willi syndrome, caused by a deletion of chromosome 15, is characterized by obesity, hyperphagia, short-stature, micromelia, hypogonadism, and mild mental retardation.

D. Lesh–Nyhan syndrome is a rare X-linked recessively inherited disease characterized by choreoathetosis, spasticity, self-mutilation, and mental retardation. This syndrome is caused by a deficiency of hypoxanthine-guanine phosphoribosyltransferase.

ANSWER 56

E. Tourette's disorder, a condition defined by the presence of multiple motor tics, and at least one vocal tic, is often effectively treated with haloperidol.

A. Agents decreasing central dopaminergic activity, including methylphenidate, amphetamines, pemoline, and cocaine, tend to exacerbate tics.

B. Around 50% of people with Tourette's disorder also have ADHD, and around 40% of them also have OCD.

C. Psychotherapy may be helpful for dealing with the consequences of the illness, such as social stigma, but is unlikely to impact on the symptoms themselves. Various forms of behavioral therapy have been studied in Tourette's disorder, including self-monitoring, habit reversal treatment, and other methods, but none have been found particularly effective.

D. Clonidine, a central alpha-2 agonist, is an effective treatment for Tourette's disorder.

ANSWER 57

B. Schizoid personality disorder is characterized by a persistent pattern of detachment from close relationships and indifference to praise or criticism by others beginning in early adulthood. The individual has a restricted range of expressing emotions in social or interpersonal situations, thus appears cold and detached. These individuals prefer solitary activities and appear socially isolated.

A. Schizotypal personality disorder is characterized by a persistent pattern of social and interpersonal deficits associated with perceptual distortions and eccentricities of behavior. These individuals lack close friends or confidants due to their discomfort with interpersonal situations, rather than lacking a desire for intimacy.

C. Avoidant personality disorder is characterized by a persistent pattern of social inhibition and feelings of inadequacy in social situations. There is a lack of intimate relationships due to a fear of being embarrassed, rejected, or found inadequate by others.

D. Obsessive–compulsive personality disorder is characterized by a persistent pattern of preoccupation with perfectionism, orderliness, and mental and interpersonal control. These individuals are preoccupied with logic and intellect and have difficulty expressing warm emotions. Social detachment often results from an excessive devotion to work.

ANSWER 58

B. Without a release of information from the patient, this would be a breach of confidentiality. She should be asked to sign a release first. Should she refuse, of course, this would suggest she was malingering to obtain alprazolam, which is a medication with considerable abuse potential.

A. Many patients with panic disorder complain of side effects when started on the usual doses of medications but do quite well with low doses titrated up slowly.

C. A limited prescription of alprazolam is justifiable. 2 mg tid is approximately the mean dose which studies have found to be effective in patients with panic disorder, despite it being higher than most doctors actually prescribe.

D. This is a typical starting dose for patients with panic disorder. Although patients on benzodiazepines do have a risk of seizure if their dose is suddenly lowered, she has already been without medication for 2 weeks. Alprazolam's half-life is only 12 hours, and thus she is past the period of high risk for a seizure.

E. Many clinicians consider this the preferred benzodiazepine for patients with panic disorder because of its long half-life and high potency.

ANSWER 59

E. Patients with double depression are about 3 times more likely to develop hypomania than are patients with episodic major depressive disorder.

A. Double depression is relatively common, occurring in 25–50% of all patients with major depressive disorder.

B. Risk of suicide is higher in double depression.

C. Double depression is more treatment-resistant than episodic major depressive disorder.

D. Double depression refers to a dysthymic disorder with a superimposed major depressive disorder.

ANSWER 60

D. All of the above.

In Alzheimer's dementia the most obvious finding is the progressive loss of memory for recent events. Problems with executive functions and changes in personality may also occur.

ANSWER 61

D. Encouraging discussion of past events in remote memory has not been shown to be of benefit in maintaining cognitive function or improving behavior when compared to placebo.

A. Orienting a person to time, place, situation, and person reduces behavioral problems and improves cognition.

B. Cognitive function has shown improvements with gingko biloba compared to placebo in randomized control trials and with better tolerance than there often is with other pharmaceuticals.

C. Improvements in cognitive function have been seen in comparisons to placebo in randomized control trials for patients taking the acetylcholine-esterase inhibitor donepezil.

E. In randomized control trials benefits are seen in comparison to placebo in cognition, behavior, and mood for early dementia patients taking the monoamine oxidase inhibitor selegiline.

ANSWER 62

D. Gender identity begins to evolve in early childhood and appears to be firmly established by about 18 months of age. Gender identity is not the same as gender role, which refers to the expectations, attitudes, or behaviors of men and women in a particular society. Gender identity is also influenced by cultural factors.

ANSWER 63

C. Typically grief is associated with social withdrawal, inertia, and loss of interest. Somatic symptoms often seen in acute grief response include loss of appetite, tightness in the throat and chest, abdominal emptiness, and fatigue. In this case, where there was no warning, the period of disability may be prolonged and intense.

ANSWER 64

Numbered phases and answers:

A. 1. Sexual aversion. Disorders of desire also include hypoactive and hypersexuality.

D. 2. Erectile dysfunction or impotence. Phase 2 disorders in women include poor vaginal lubrication, dyspareunia, and vaginismus.

B. 3. Premature ejaculation.

C. 4. Retrograde ejaculation; delayed orgasm and anorgasmia are also associated with this phase of sexual response.

E. 5. Priapism is the male sexual dysfunction associated with the resolution phase.

ANSWER 65

D. All of the above.

Although there are no consistent medication treatments for the various personality disorders, many studies have found benefit in treating symptom clusters within and across disorders as well as treating the associated axis I disorders. Individuals with intermittent symptoms may benefit from taking medications as needed, during prodromal symptoms or times of increased stress.

BLOCK **THREE**

QUESTIONS

Setting 3: In-Patient Facilities

You have general admitting privileges to the hospital. You may see patients in the critical care unit or the pediatrics unit or the maternity unit or in recovery. You may also be called to see patients in the psychiatric unit. There is a short-stay unit for patients undergoing same-day operations or being held for observation. There are adjacent nursing home/extended-care facilities and a detoxification unit where you may see patients.

QUESTION 66

A 78-year-old retired coal miner has been transferred to the ICU from a general medical ward. Three days later there is a change in his cognition with disturbed consciousness and impaired speech.

Each of the following statements about delirium is true EXCEPT:

A. ICU patients tend to have no discernable organic etiology explaining their delirium.

B. A prodrome is common.

C. Elderly patients are at higher risk for developing a delirium.

D. Postcardiotomy patients are at higher risk for developing a delirium.

E. There is a higher mortality rate.

QUESTION 67

Each of the following is an appropriate treatment intervention for the hospitalized elderly patient with delirium EXCEPT:

A. Place a clock, calendar, and familiar objects in the room.

B. Establish close supervision by reassuring nursing staff and family.

C. Place the patient in a room with another delirious patient to minimize supervision.

D. Prescribe haloperidol at 0.5–2 mg for agitation.

E. Reverse the suspected etiology.

QUESTION 68

As a psychiatric consultant for the general hospital, the nursing supervisor of an adjacent nursing home asks you to provide an inservice to her staff on depression in the elderly.

The prevalence of late-life depressive disorders in long-term care facilities is typically in which one of the following ranges?

A. 1–3%

B. 10–15%

C. 33–56%

D. 90–100%

E. None of the above

QUESTION 69

A 43-year-old school teacher develops signs and symptoms of delirium 4 days after receiving a kidney transplant. A psychiatric consultation is requested.

Which one of the following immunosuppressants is capable of causing delirium?

A. Cyclosporin A (CyA)

B. FK 506

C. OKT3

D. All of the above

E. None of the above

QUESTION 70

A 73-year-old woman with ovarian cancer is admitted to the surgical service for evaluation of acute abdominal pain. A psychiatric consultation is requested because the patient also has a psychiatric illness.

Which one of the following statements regarding the expected length of stay for this particular patient is TRUE?

A. Presence of a psychiatric illness is associated with a longer hospitalization.

B. Older age is associated with a longer hospitalization.

C. A diagnosis of a neoplasm is associated with a longer hospitalization.

D. All of the above.

E. None of the above.

QUESTION 71

The charge nurse of the short-stay unit at the hospital related that frequently patients are admitted intoxicated and have been taking mood-stabilizing medications for their bipolar illness. She asks you to write down a simple chart for her staff about these medications.

Match the psychotropic medication with its accepted therapeutic levels.

A. Lithium carbonate

B. Valproic acid

C. Carbamazepine

1. 50–125 μg/ml

2. 0.8–1.2 mEq/L

3. 4.0–12.0 mg/L

QUESTION 72

A 24-year-old female is admitted for evaluation of new-onset psychotic symptoms. Two weeks ago she began to experience auditory and visual hallucinations, paranoid ideas, restlessness, sleep disruption, and confusion. She has a 2-year history of dependence on heroin and benzodiazepines, including intravenous drug use. On examination, she is thought-disordered and her Mini-Mental State Examination score is 17 out of 30 with deficits in attention and short-term memory. She has a pulse rate of 110 but is afebrile. A contrast-enhanced MRI image of her brain is seen below. Which of the following statements about her condition is FALSE?

A. Electroencephalographic (EEG) studies can usually differentiate delirium from primary psychotic disorders.

B. Haloperidol is indicated both for patients with primary psychotic disorders and those with delirium.

C. Her treatment regime should include benzodiazepine.

D. Absence of fever is unusual with brain abscesses.

E. Deficits in memory occur more often in delirium than in primary psychotic disorders.

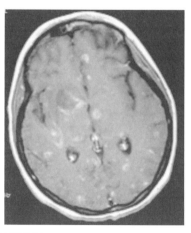

FIGURE 72

QUESTION 73

A 44-year-old woman is admitted to the hospital for treatment of mania. This is her first manic episode. She also has hepatitis C. Which of the following medications would be the most appropriate for mood stabilization?

A. Valproic acid

B. Lithium

C. Carbamazepine

D. Clonazepam

E. Gabapentin

QUESTION 74

The nursing staff of the extended-care facility where you consult frequently asks you to develop an inservice about the management of demented patients. They are particularly interested in learning some nonpharmacologic strategies.

Treating the behavioral manifestations of dementia include each of the following EXCEPT:

A. Frequent reorientation

B. Securing doors

C. Activity during daytime hours

D. Limiting fluid intake at night

E. Providing a stimulating environment

QUESTION 75

A psychiatric consultation is requested to evaluate a 44-year-old male, hospitalized for treatment of multiple brain abscesses and a secondary left hemiparesis, for behavioral problems. He has been exposing himself to other patients, making crude remarks, and shouting requests for lobster for lunch at the nursing staff. On examination, his affect is jovial and he says that he feels happy that there is nothing wrong with him, and that he doesn't need to be in the hospital. He tells the psychiatrist, who is bald, jokes ridiculing bald people. He interprets the proverb, "People who live in glass houses shouldn't throw stones," as meaning, "They would break the glass." When asked to copy figures, he produces the following responses:

The signs and symptoms he displays include all of the following EXCEPT:

A. Concreteness

B. Witzelsucht

C. Perseveration

D. Anosognosia

E. Alexithymia

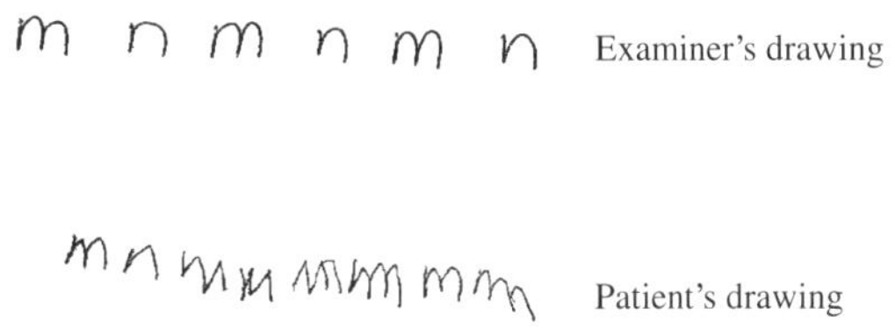

Examiner's drawing

Patient's drawing

FIGURE 75

QUESTION 76

A 24-year-old male is admitted to the hospital for new-onset psychosis. A college student, who has no previous psychiatric history, has done well in classes, and had been asymptomatic until 2 weeks prior to admission. At that time he developed paranoid ideation and auditory hallucinations. These were followed by insomnia and depressed mood. On admission, his affect is blunted, his speech is disorganized, and he complains of ongoing auditory hallucinations, but he is alert and fully oriented. A workup for organic causes of psychosis including an MRI of the brain is negative.

All of the following features are suggestive of a good prognosis in this patient EXCEPT:

A. Short duration of symptoms

B. Clear sensorium

C. Affective symptoms

D. Lack of structural brain abnormalities

E. Good premorbid functioning

QUESTIONS 77–81

The nursing staff of the general medical floor at the hospital is frequently perplexed in working with patients described by the attendings as having personality disorders. The nurses ask you to provide a straightforward inservice differentiating the various types of personality disorders.

For each specified personality disorder, select the expected patterns of behavior as described below.

A. Antisocial personality disorder

B. Schizoid personality disorder

C. Histrionic personality disorder

D. Borderline personality disorder

E. Avoidant personality disorder

QUESTION 77

Solitary lifestyle by choice, indifferent to others, and emotionally detached.

QUESTION 78

Consistently irresponsible, indifferent to mistreatment of others, and deceitfulness.

QUESTION 79

Unstable, intense personal relationships with affective instability, and impulsivity.

QUESTION 80

Hypersensitivity to evaluation by others, social inhibition, and feeling inadequate.

QUESTION 81

Sexually provocative, shallow emotions, and suggestibility.

QUESTION 82

During teaching rounds with a group of third-year medical students on the inpatient unit, one of the students asks you to explain how malpractice is defined in psychiatry.

Psychiatric malpractice includes which of the following?

A. A duty to care for the patient

B. A dereliction of this duty

C. A direct relationship between the dereliction and damage to the patient

D. The presence of damage

E. All of the above

BLOCK THREE

ANSWERS

ANSWER 66

A. When pursued, over 80% of ICU patients with a delirium have a clear organic etiology.

B & C. Those confused related to psychological or environmental events are typically severely demented.

D. Burn patients, those with decreased cerebral reserve due to stroke, and patients in drug withdrawal are also at high risk to develop delirium.

E. Elderly patients developing a delirium in the hospital have a 20–75% chance of dying during that hospitalization.

ANSWER 67

C. A common mistake on medical and surgical floors is to have delirious patients share the same room. This makes reorientation nearly impossible and they may confirm with each other their misperceptions.

A & B. Although sometimes helpful, environmental interventions are not a primary treatment; calm, reassuring family and staff can prevent mishaps for the confused patient.

D. The usual starting dose to control agitation in the elderly patient is in the lower range when using medications such as haloperidol.

E. The goal of diagnosis and treatment of delirium is to correct reversible causes.

ANSWER 68

C. 33–56%.

Symptoms of depression are relatively common in the elderly population. Considering broad depressive symptoms, the prevalence in the community-base elderly over 65 years old is in the 16–32% range. The prevalence is even higher for elderly residents of assisted-care or long-term care facilities. Although symptoms of depression are common among the elderly, it is not a normal part of aging and should not be accepted as such.

ANSWER 69

D. All of the above.

Most immunosuppressants are capable of causing delirium as well as other neuropsychiatric disorders. CyA is a commonly used immunosuppressant that inhibits interleukin-2. It is associated with delirium when levels exceed 1,000 ng/ml persistently. Trough plasma levels above 3 ng/ml of FK 506 are associated with delirium as well. The delirium seen with OKT3 tends to be transient and associated with each bolus therapy. Lowering the dose of the offending immunosuppressant usually reduces the recurrence of delirium.

ANSWER 70

D. All of the above.

Older age, a diagnosis of neoplasm, number of all physical diagnoses, the number of previous nonpsychiatric hospital admissions and the presence of certain psychiatric disorders predict an increased length of stay. In particular dementia, substance abuse disorders, and psychiatric illnesses secondary to alcohol and drug abuse show a significantly increased length of stay.

ANSWER 71

B. 50–125 μg/ml

Valproic acid. In placebo-controlled clinical trials of acute mania, patients were successfully dosed to a clinical response with trough plasma concentrations between these levels.

A. 0.8–1.2 mEq/L

Lithium carbonate has a relatively narrow therapeutic range with limited efficacy below 0.8 mEq/L and toxicity over 1.5 mEq/L.

C. 4.0–12.0 mg/L

Carbamazepine. The reference range for therapeutic efficacy is the same for this medication's anticonvulsant use. It can be potentially toxic above 12 mg/L.

ANSWER 72

D. Fever is present in only 45–50% of patients with brain abscesses. Absence of fever should not be used to exclude the diagnosis.

A. EEG is usually abnormal in delirium, whereas it is usually normal in primary psychotic disorders like schizophrenia.

B. This is true. Haloperidol is frequently used to control agitation in delirium.

C. A benzodiazepine would be useful to prevent or treat withdrawal in this patient.

E. Deficits in attention, orientation or memory are more suggestive of delirium or dementia than of a primary psychotic disorder.

ANSWER 73

B. Lithium is the treatment of choice for classic euphoric mania. In some forms of bipolar disorder, such as dysphoric mania, mania with psychosis, and rapid cycling, valproic acid is considered the treatment of choice. However, when liver disease is comorbid with these forms of bipolar disorder, lithium is the treatment of choice. Unlike valproic acid, lithium is renally excreted and is not metabolized by the liver.

A, C, & D. These medications are metabolized by the liver.

E. Like lithium, gabapentin is not metabolized by the liver and is renally excreted. Nevertheless, it is not believed to be as effective a mood stabilizer as lithium, so it is not a first-line agent.

ANSWER 74

E. A stimulating or changing environment tends to be overly distracting or confusing to someone with dementia. Efforts should be made to avoid change and provide consistency.

A. Frequent reorientation through personal contact and placement of calendars and clocks can be helpful.

B. Safety is always a concern and doors should be secured as a deterrent for the wandering patient.

C & D. Activity during the daytime and fluid restriction as the evening approaches may both promote improved sleep at night.

ANSWER 75

E. Alexithymia is defined as a difficulty in identifying or describing one's feelings. It is classically seen in patients with somatization disorder who typically express emotional distress in terms of physical symptoms.

A. The patient's proverb interpretation demonstrates concreteness of thought. He was unable to see the metaphorical meaning of the proverb.

B. Witzelsucht refers to an inappropriate jocularity and insensitive humor, often displayed by patients with frontal lobe pathology.

C. Perseveration, an abnormal continuation of behavior, is a common feature of frontal lobe pathology and is seen in this patient's attempts to copy the examiner's figures. He produced extra arches on his "m"s and "n"s.

D. Anosognosia is the denial of illness, typically seen with right parietal lobe pathology.

ANSWER 76

B. A clear sensorium during psychotic episodes is a negative prognostic factor. This is because delirium-like confusion is more often associated with the transient psychoses such as brief psychotic disorder or postpartum psychosis than it is with schizophrenia.

A, C, D, & E. These are all suggestive of a good prognosis.

ANSWER 77

B. Schizoid personality disorder.

These individuals are often perceived as strange or eccentric but usually do not have prominent paranoia.

ANSWER 78

A. Antisocial personality disorder.

This disorder may become less evident as the individual ages. It is more common in males.

ANSWER 79

D. Borderline personality disorder.

This disorder is 5 times more common among first-degree relatives of those with the disorder.

ANSWER 80

E. Avoidant personality disorder.

ANSWER 81

C. Histrionic personality disorder.

Many individuals may display histrionic personality traits and several of the characteristics are shared with other personality disorders. A personality disorder implies an enduring cognitive, affective, interpersonal, and impulse control pattern usually traced back to adolescence or early adulthood. The patterns are inflexible and deviate significantly from the individual's cultural norms and are not accounted for by another mental disorder, a general medical condition or the effects of a chemical substance. Many personality disorders have mixed features.

ANSWER 82

E. All of the above.

The four "D"s of medical malpractice include duty, dereliction, direct cause, and damages. Generally there must be proof by a preponderance of the evidence that these components are present and the result of professional negligence.

BLOCK FOUR

QUESTIONS

Setting 4: Emergency Department

Generally patients encountered here are seeking urgent care and most are not known to you. Available to you are a full range of social services, including rape crisis intervention, family support, child protective services, domestic violence support, psychiatric services, and security assistance backed up by local police. Complete laboratory and radiology services are available.

QUESTION 83

A 26-year-old single woman presents to the emergency center relating that over the past four nights she has been awakened by discrete episodes of a palpitating heart, choking sensations, sweating, trembling, and derealization. She is petrified that another episode may occur.

Which of the following is the most likely psychiatric diagnosis?

A. Specific phobia

B. Panic attack

C. Performance anxiety

D. All of the above

E. None of the above

QUESTION 84

How often is agoraphobia associated with panic disorder?

A. Nearly 100% of the time

B. 10% of the time

C. One-third of the time

D. Never

E. None of the above

QUESTION 85

Which one of the following psychiatric syndromes is associated with panic disorder?

A. Major depression

B. Personality disorders

C. Alcoholism

D. All of the above

E. None of the above

QUESTION 86

Each of the following medications is useful in treating panic disorder EXCEPT:

A. Sertraline

B. Citalopram

C. Fluoxetine

D. Paroxetine

E. Olanzapine

QUESTION 87

A 62-year-old man presents to the emergency center with sudden loss of speech. His family tells you that he is a right-handed man who while at the dinner table suddenly dropped the fork from his hand. They noticed a drooping of the right side of his face, unsteady gait favoring the right leg, and inability to communicate verbally with them. He follows your instructions in the exam, but a noticeable strength deficit is present in the right face, arm, and hand. His speech is minimal with a telegraphic quality and diffuse grammatical errors. Though many areas may be affected by this patient's stroke, which area below would characteristically explain his difficulties speaking?

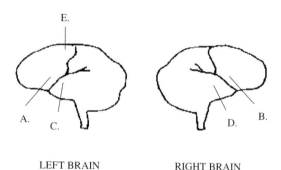

LEFT BRAIN   RIGHT BRAIN

FIGURE 87

QUESTION 88

A 33-year-old woman was brought to the emergency center by her husband for evaluation of a broken leg. The husband reports that she had tripped and fallen down the stairs. On physical exam, you notice there are multiple bruises on her chest, back, and abdomen. You ask the husband to leave the examining room and ask the patient if there has been any domestic violence at home. She hesitantly admits that her husband hits her when there is an argument between them. Which of the following would be the most appropriate intervention?

A. Encourage the patient to stand up to her husband and threaten to leave him if he hits her again.

B. Tell the patient that spousal abuse is grounds for divorce and that she should leave him.

C. Report the husband to the police and have him arrested.

D. Have a social worker involved to educate the patient on domestic violence and give her a list of shelters where she can go if she feels her life is in danger.

E. Arrange for the patient and her husband to have marital counseling.

QUESTION 89

A 78-year-old man is brought to the emergency center by his wife because he is confused. He has had no memory impairment in the past, but this morning he couldn't remember what year it was or what city they live in. He has difficulty staying awake for the interview, but his wife states he was up frequently last night to urinate. He becomes irritable and pulls out his intravenous lines in the emergency room and accuses the nursing staff of trying to rob him. Which of the following should you recommend?

A. Admission to the psychiatric unit to rule out schizophrenia.

B. Admission to the psychiatric unit to rule out dementia.

C. Outpatient evaluation for dementia.

D. Initiate a medical workup with physical or chemical restraints used if needed for his safety.

E. None of the above.

QUESTION 90

A 27-year-old Asian man was visiting his family in the United States and is brought to the emergency center for suicidal ideation. The patient fears his penis is shrinking and disappearing into his abdomen and he feels he is going to die. He has had no previous psychiatric history. You reassure the family and the patient that an antipsychotic medication will help and that his symptoms are consistent with a culturally based psychotic disorder known as:

A. Amok

B. Schizophreniform

C. Koro

D. Autoerotic asphyxiation

E. None of the above

QUESTION 91

A 16-year-old girl is brought to the emergency center by several friends because she has become agitated at a social gathering they were all attending. On examination she is very anxious with noticeable skin excoriations, dilated pupils, bronchospasms, and a rapid heart beat.

Which one of the following substances is most likely related to this patient's clinical presentation?

A. Alcohol

B. Opiates

C. Marijuana

D. Cocaine

E. None of the above

QUESTION 92

Which is the usual length of time cocaine is detectable in the urine?

A. 8 days

B. 4 weeks

C. 72 hours

D. 6–8 hours

E. None of the above

QUESTION 93

An overdose of the drug ecstasy can result in which of the following?

A. Hypertension

B. Panic attacks

C. Seizures

D. Hyperthermia

E. All of the above

QUESTION 94

A 23-year-old single male is brought to the emergency center by the paramedics after his family called 911. They feared the patient overdosed on his prescribed lithium. The patient is lethargic, tremulous, and confused.

Each of the following statements about lithium is true EXCEPT:

A.   Therapeutic level is 0.6–1.2 mEq/L.

B.   Toxic level is typically more than 2.0 mEq/L.

C.   Half-life of lithium is 48–60 hours.

D.   Toxic levels can cause stupor, coma, and death.

E.   None of the above.

QUESTION 95

Besides impaired renal function, which of the following is a cause of increased lithium levels?

A.   Dehydration

B.   Ibuprofen

C.   Thiazides

D.   Sodium restriction

E.   All of the above

QUESTION 96

An 88-year-old widower was transferred from his nursing home to the emergency center. The patient had a history of recurrent depression since age 54, with the most recent episode occurring 18 months ago. At that time he was successfully treated with the SSRI sertraline and he remained on that medication. One week prior to the admission, the patient became agitated in the nursing home and was started on haloperidol and benzotropine. The past few days he had become drowsy but arousable and disoriented. Physical examination was normal except for a blood pressure of 94/60 and a pulse of 92. He appeared dehydrated. Laboratory studies were unremarkable except for a white blood cell count of 12,000 mm^3 and a cloudy urinalysis with 3+ bacteria.

Each of the following is indicated in the acute care of the patient EXCEPT:

A.   Discontinue the haloperidol.

B.   Discontinue the benzotropine.

C.   Treat the urinary tract infection.

D.   Hydrate the patient.

E.   All of the above.

QUESTION 97

An 18-year-old male high school student presents to the emergency center with a variety of unusual symptoms. After a physical examination, including vital signs, and a screening neurological examination are found to be normal, you are consulted as the on-call psychiatrist. After listening to the history again, you recommend an MRI of the brain. The noncontrast MRI image appears below.

Based on the location of the brain tumor, which of the following symptom clusters was the patient most likely to have been experiencing?

A. Sudden rampage, including suicidal and homicidal behavior, ending in exhaustion and amnesia.

B. Visual, auditory, and olfactory hallucinations, déjà vu, automatisms, forced thinking.

C. Poor concentration, inability to generate or carry out plans, trouble with sequencing tasks, attention deficit, indifference to consequences.

D. Right-left disorientation, inability to localize fingers, agraphia, acalculia.

E. Visual agnosia, apathy, placidity, disturbed sexual function, aphasia, amnesia.

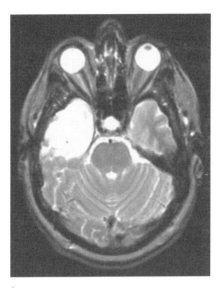

FIGURE 97

QUESTION 98

A 14-year-old patient you are seeing in the emergency center has bruises in various stages of healing all over her body. The patient becomes very tearful when asked about her bruises. Her mother is out of the room when the patient tells you that she is being sexually and physically abused at home. She asks you not to say anything to anyone including her mother and the authorities. What do you say?

A. "I am obligated by law to report this situation to the authorities."

B. "I must tell your mother because she is your guardian, but it is her choice whether the authorities are involved."

C. "Though I can't break your confidentiality, I will need to document this situation in your chart."

D. All of the above.

E. None of the above.

QUESTION 99

The nursing staff of the emergency center asks you to develop an inservice to help them deal with dangerous patients.

Each of the following statements regarding the assessment of violent patients is true EXCEPT:

A. Have assistance nearby.

B. Place yourself between the patient and the exit.

C. Seek the patient's alliance.

D. Allow the patient to ventilate.

E. None of the above.

QUESTION 100

An over-talkative, hyperactive 63-year-old man is triaged by the emergency center nurse for a psychiatric consultation.

Which of the following medications DO NOT have a propensity to cause manic symptoms?

A. Levodopa

B. Tricyclic antidepressants

C. Decongestants

D. Isoniazid

E. None of the above

BLOCK **FOUR**

ANSWERS

ANSWER 83

B. Panic attacks are defined as fear or discomfort that arises abruptly—even during deep sleep—and peaks in 10 minutes or less. Symptoms include those listed above as well as rapid or labored breathing, chest pain, nausea, light headedness or dizziness, numbing or tingling of extremities, a sense of unreality, and chills or hot flashes.

A. Specific phobias include fears of something specific such as spiders or flying.

C. Performance anxiety is associated with public speaking.

ANSWER 84

C. In about one-third of cases, panic attacks lead to agoraphobia. The definition of agoraphobia is an anticipatory anxiety about being in a situation where either escape or help are unavailable if an attack should occur. The persistent fear about future attacks can be very disabling and demoralizing.

ANSWER 85

D. All of the above.

Two-thirds of those with panic disorder have another psychiatric disorder. About half have a history of major depression. Men in particular have alcohol and drug problems; some presumably trying to medicate themselves. The anxious cluster personality disorders of avoidant, dependent, and obsessive–compulsive are also related to panic disorder.

ANSWER 86

E. Olanzapine, an antipsychotic, is not helpful in treating panic disorder.

A, B, C, & D. The selective serotonin reuptake inhibitors (SSRIs) such as sertraline, citalopram, fluoxetine, and paroxetine have become the preferred pharmacologic intervention. Because they may increase anxiety somewhat at first they are generally started at doses lower than used for treating depression. Since it may be weeks before the SSRIs become effective, benzodiazepines are often used in the interim.

ANSWER 87

A. This is Broca's area, which is represented in Broadman's schematic as area 44. This is the area of the brain where language is produced fluently with grammatical proficiency. Since this patient is right-handed with right-sided motor deficits on exam, the left brain is the location of the lesion.

B. This is a possible explanation of this patient's loss of speech if he were one of the few (1%) right-handed people who has left brain dominance.

C. This is Wernicke's area, which corresponds to Broadman's area 22. Werneke's aphasia involves poor comprehension of speech. Production of speech is nonsensical but has fluidity and grammar.

D. Again the dominant hemisphere is the location of the speech center, and this person has a 99% chance that this should be left-sided, not right-sided, as is more commonly seen in left-handed individuals (30–40%).

E. The parietal area on the right is affected and this could contribute to the difficulty making the mouth movements for normal speech. The patient's communication problem extends beyond just motor difficulties and therefore suggests that Broca's area is the more likely affected area.

ANSWER 88

D. The goal is to resolve violence, which involves participation of the spouse who is the abuser or a plan that enables the victim an opportunity to leave the abuse. Social agencies can address issues such as child custody and provide resources such as shelters that enable the battered spouse to escape the abusive situation.

A. Confrontation of the abuser often leads to further persecution or abuse of the spouse who becomes less passive toward the abuser.

B. Homelessness may be a concern for the abused spouse. Often the abused woman is fearful to leave because the abuser will intimidate her and threaten to harm her if she leaves.

C. The abuse should be reported by the victim or someone who witnesses the abuse. Calling the police may exacerbate the abuse when the woman decides to return home with her husband.

E. Although therapy may be helpful, the emergent intervention from these choices is D.

ANSWER 89

D. A patient with agitation and psychosis can be managed on a medical floor or emergency room with the same use of chemical and physical restraints as is used in the psychiatric setting. Delirium should be medically evaluated immediately and thoroughly, since many causes such as urinary tract infections, pneumonias, meningitis, renal failure, or drug ingestions can be quickly treated and reversed. If delirium is not addressed, it may progress to permanent disability or death.

A. Schizophrenia is highly unlikely due to the patient's age and the rapid onset of symptoms.

B. Dementia does not present acutely unless there is a superimposed delirium. With no prior history of memory difficulties, it is unlikely that dementia alone is the cause of this clinical presentation.

C. A dementia workup, which can include a physical exam, CBC, electrolytes, renal and liver function tests, B_{12}, folate, TSH, RPR, HIV, LP, and CT or MRI, can be done as an outpatient if the patient is stable. Delirium is not a stable condition and is considered a medical emergency.

ANSWER 90

C. There are cultural issues that must be addressed whenever a patient presents with a new onset of psychosis. An important factor in any new psychosis is whether this could be a cultural or religiously based belief or behavior. This particular syndrome, though cultural, is a psychotic disorder. It may occur in women as well, and as long as there is no premorbid history of psychosis it will likely clear in time. These patients are at risk for suicide due to the severe anxiety produced.

A. A Malayan term for furiously and suddenly engaging in battle. Persons typically are overtaken with severe homicidal ideation and often end the fury by killing themselves.

B. This is the diagnosis for an individual who presents with more than a month but less than a 6-month history of psychosis. If symptoms last less than a month, it is a brief psychotic disorder. If symptoms last longer than 6 months, it is schizophrenia.

D. Seen mostly in young men and transvestites, it involves hanging oneself while masturbating to heighten the intensity of orgasm. Often this results in unintended death.

ANSWER 91

D. Cocaine intoxication can cause anxiety and agitation as well as several physical findings associated with stimulant abuse and routes of ingestion.

A. Recent alcohol intoxication can be disinhibiting but more typically results in lethargy and ataxia.

B. Opiate intoxication results in constricted pupils.

C. A physical sign of marijuana intoxication includes congestion of the conjunctiva.

ANSWER 92

D. Cocaine can be detected in the urine 6–8 hours after the last ingestion. Its metabolites may be present up to 2–4 days.

A. Phycyclidine (PCP) may be detectible up to 8 days.

B & C. Chronic marijuana usage may be detected for several weeks and heroin up to 72 hours.

ANSWER 93

E. All of the above.

Initially synthesized in the late 1800s, ecstasy has become a popular drug of abuse. Other street names for methylenedioxymethamphetamine include MDMA, XTC, X, and ADAM. Positive or sought-after effects include decreased anxiety, an increased perception of empathy, and a suppressed need to eat, drink, or sleep. Negative experiences include nausea, tremors, teeth clenching, muscle cramping, blurred vision, and fever. An overdose can also result in loss of consciousness, temperatures as high as 110°F, and death.

ANSWER 94

C. The half-life of lithium is normally 20–24 hours. Since lithium is primarily excreted by the kidneys, impaired renal function would prolong the half-life.

ANSWER 95

E. All of the above.

The kidneys preferentially reabsorb lithium during water and sodium restriction. Many commonly prescribed medications cause increased lithium levels; some include ibuprofen, indomethacin, methyldopa, thiazide diuretics, triamterene, spirinolactone, and ACE inhibitors.

ANSWER 96

E. All of the above.

The essential treatment of a delirium is to identify and rectify the causative agents. This patient's urinary tract infection likely precipitated the delirium. His dehydration also needs to be addressed medically. There is no current need for the antipsychotic haloperidol or the anticholinergic medication benztropine, both of which may be adding to his confused state.

ANSWER 97

B. These are common symptoms of temporal lobe lesions.

A. This describes "amok," a cultural-bound syndrome from Southeast Asia and Malaysia.

C. These are symptoms of frontal lobe impairment.

D. This is the Gerstmann syndrome, produced by dominant parietal lobe diseases.

E. This is the Klüver–Bucy syndrome, produced by *bilateral* temporal lobe lesions.

ANSWER 98

A. Any report or suspicion of child abuse or neglect must be reported to the authorities.

B. It is not sufficient to inform the mother since she could be the abuser. Your obligation is to the child and her safety.

C. Confidentiality does not apply in this situation since harm to the child is the issue. The patient should also know that the mother has the right to request a copy of any records.

ANSWER 99

B. A priority in assessing the violent patient is to prevent harm to yourself, the patient, and others. It is best to have a prepared plan and practiced training. Always allow an exit for you as well as the patient. Avoid excessive eye contact since this can be construed as threatening, disarm, and disrobe the patient, and conduct the exam in an area free from dangerous objects. If the situation deteriorates leave the room and seek help from security and other staff.

ANSWER 100

E. Drugs and medications are the most common precipitant of secondary mania. Those with a latent bipolar illness are at highest risk.

A, B, & C. Levodopa, tricyclic antidepressants, and decongestants have a direct affect on the monoamine neurotransmitters associated with mood disorders.

D. The antituberculin medication isoniazid also affects serotonin and neurepinephrine metabolism through its monoamine oxidase inhibitor properties.